AF480917

October 2024
979-8-9887655-4-7

Creatures
of the
Coast

written & illustrated by

Alexandra Sclafani

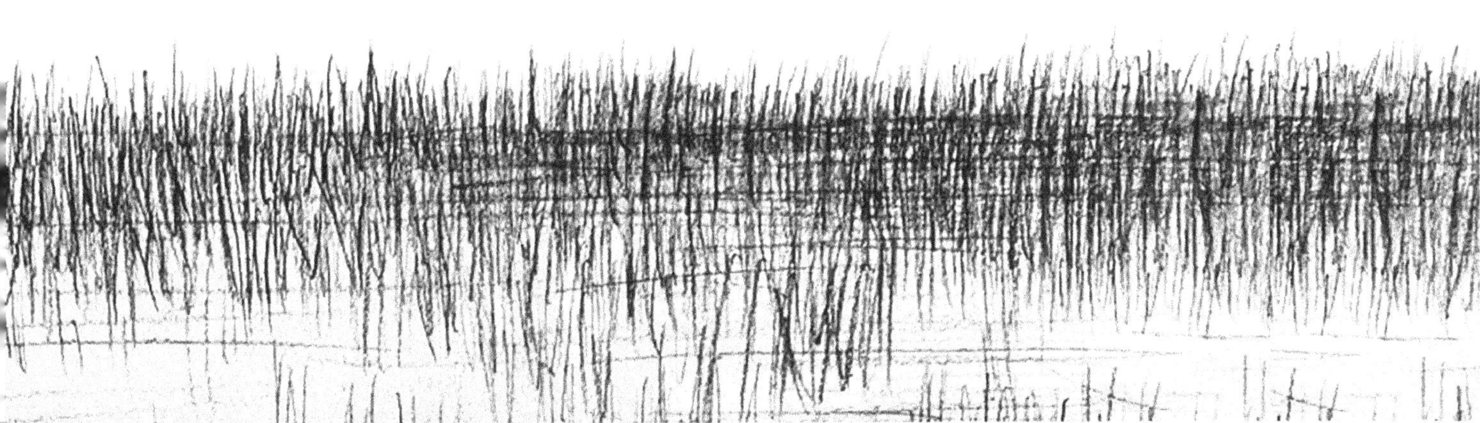

Dedicated to the magic in all things

- including the magic in you.

I call to the *aumakua*,
        on Polynesean coasts!
Reveal to me by this decree
        your presence in new host.

        If you become the Loggerhead
                who swims beneath my bow
        As you leave, I will believe
                        in what you tell me now!

Should I plan to travel far
        or adventure the next day,
        I do invite a wretched plight
                that may impact my way.

But if I wait another sun,
The *momoa* in my canoe
shall unravel assured travel,
the entire journey through.

LOGGERHEAD TURTLE

LETTERED OLIVE

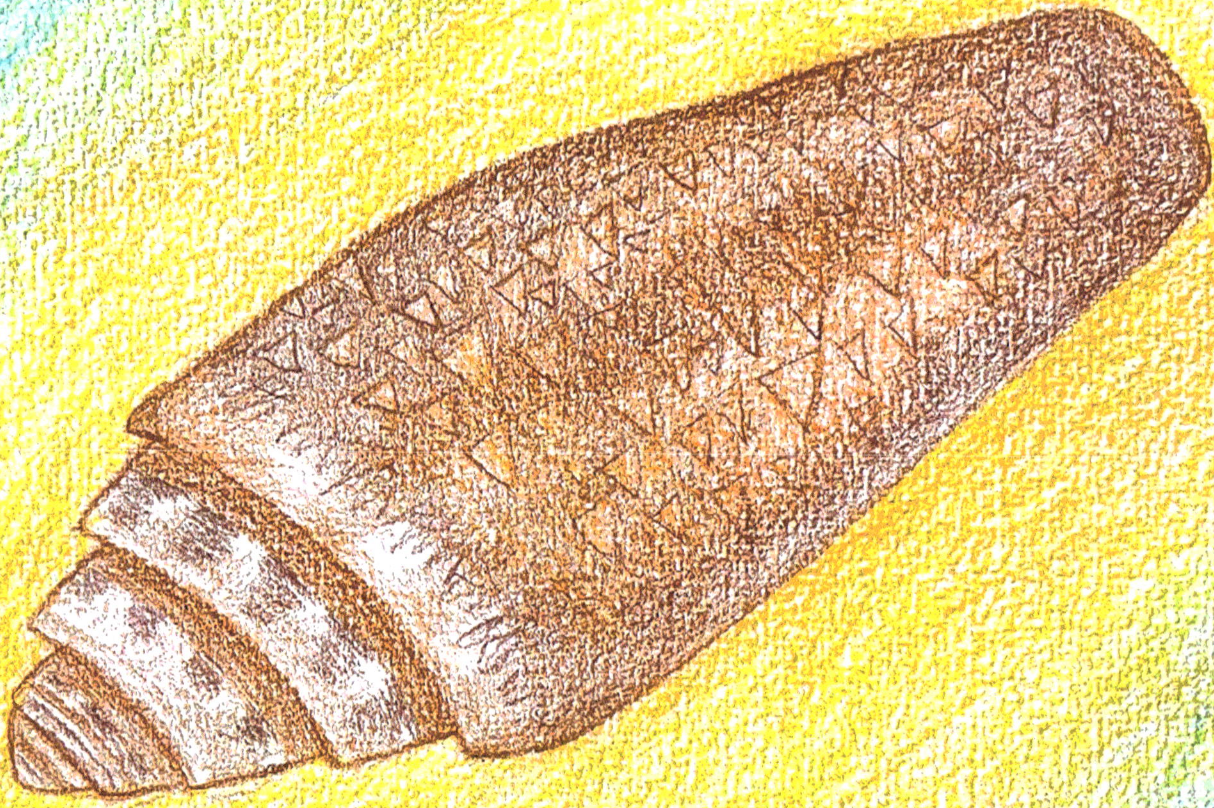

Retrieve a Lettered Olive -
on its shell a language lost!
It'll guide you forth with clarity
when words are at a loss.

A message from the ocean,
a morning spring wind brings
When you see a Great Blue Heron
sunning out her blue-gray wings.

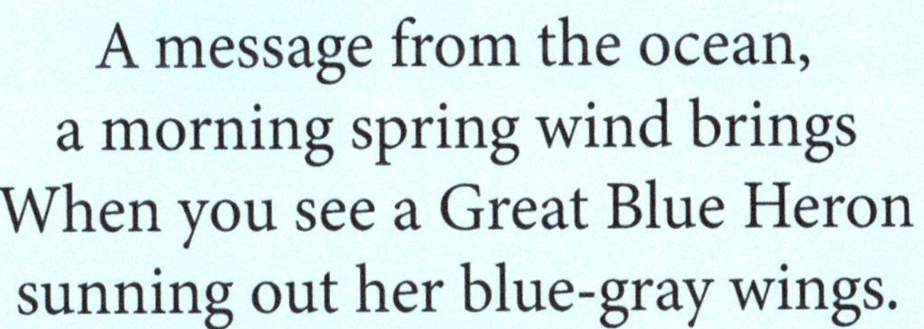

When dark storms
loom just ahead
and this messenger
appears...
on this day,
she heard you pray.
Resolution
soon is near.

GREAT BLUE HERON

Beware this scaly monster,
who is an agitator!
This ancient foe waiting below
They call the Alligator.

Find yourself on
open seas and plunge
beneath the waves.
Still your mind
and wait a time
to find the
Manta Ray...

Should you see
the winged beast
appear beneath
the surf,

The Manta Ray
will show the way.
Salvation soon
is yours.

MANTA RAY

CANNONBALL JELLYFISH

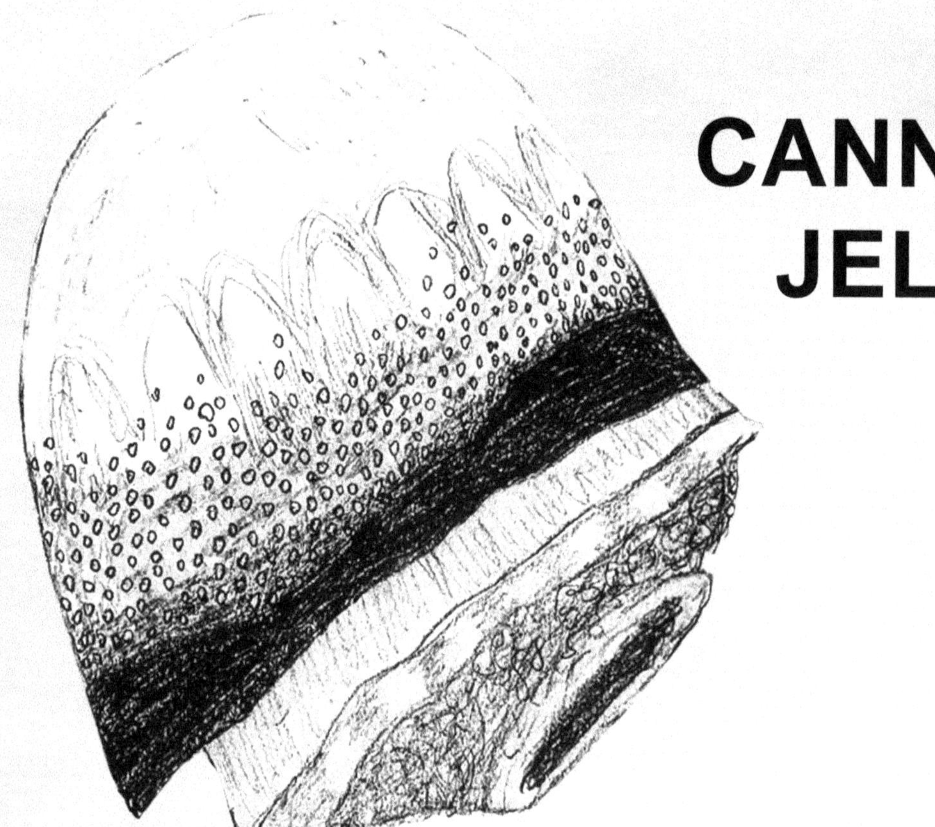

I am a many-mouthed hunter,
who needs no legs to stand!
I decide what I am to be,
the true maker of who I am.

I am the Cannonball Jellyfish,
swimming legless as I breathe...
despite size, I improvise!
No matter who believes.

MANATEE

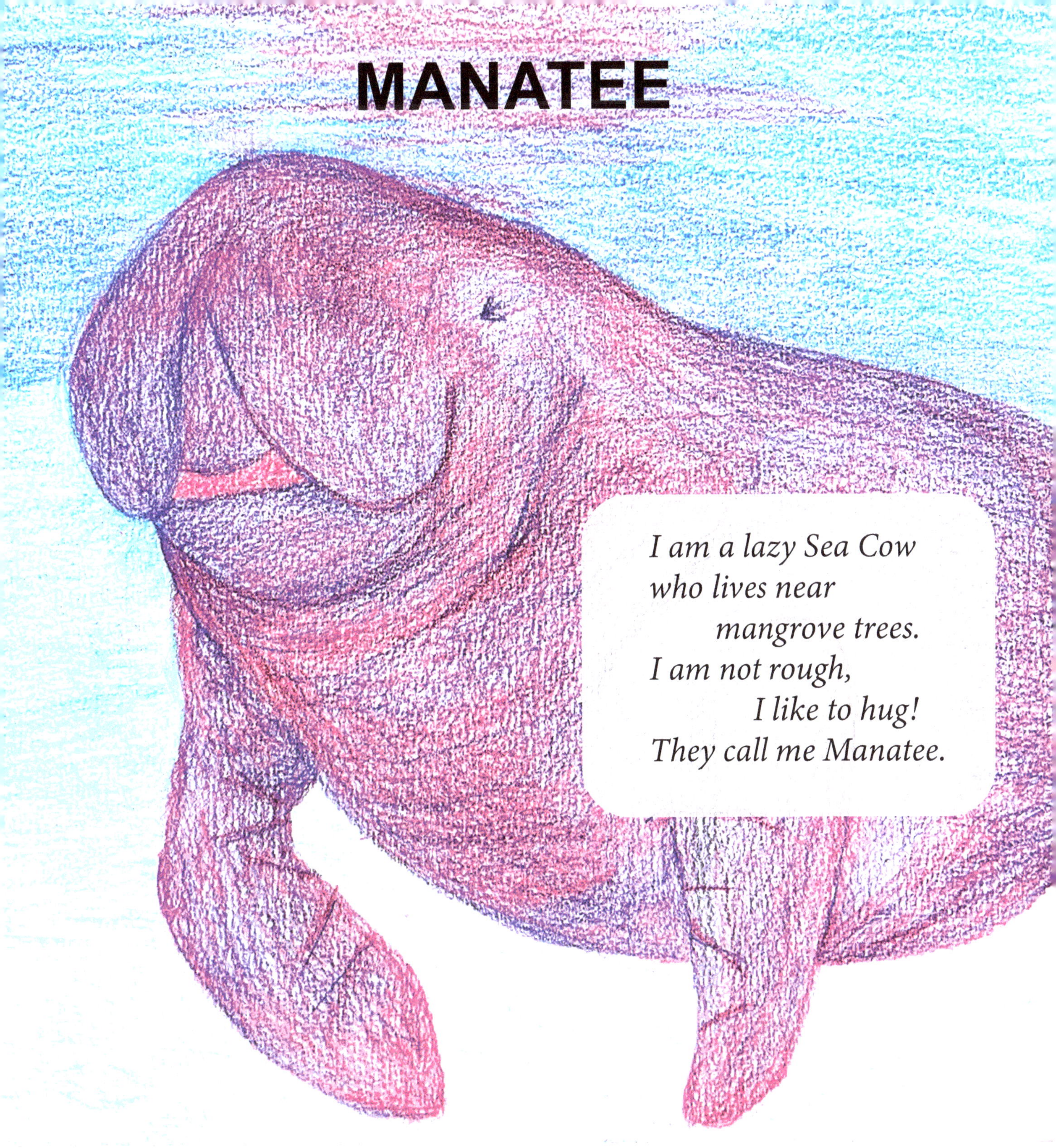

I am a lazy Sea Cow
who lives near
   mangrove trees.
I am not rough,
   I like to hug!
They call me Manatee.

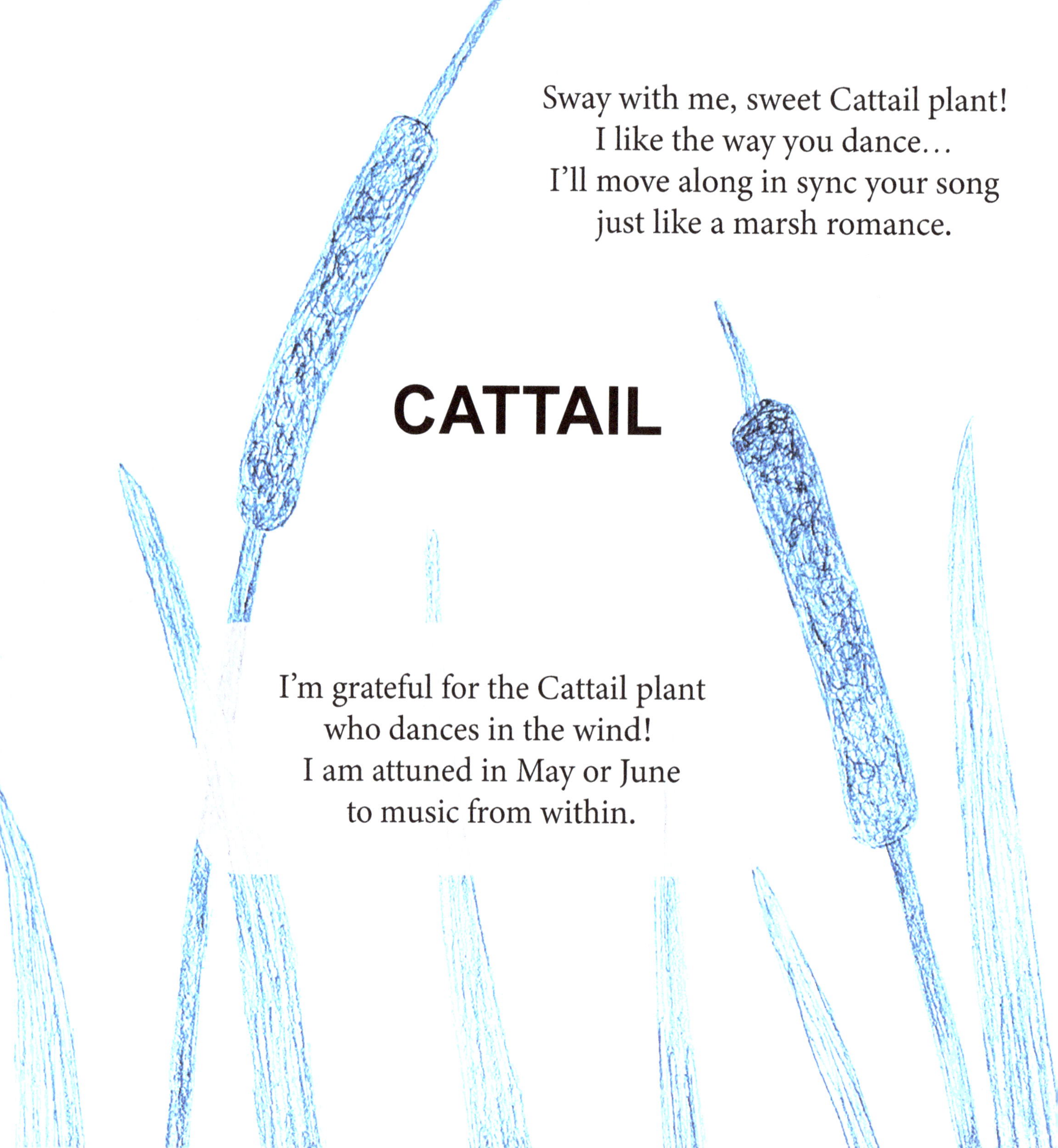

Sway with me, sweet Cattail plant!
I like the way you dance…
I'll move along in sync your song
just like a marsh romance.

CATTAIL

I'm grateful for the Cattail plant
who dances in the wind!
I am attuned in May or June
to music from within.

The Hammerhead is a friend -
a face most unmistakable.
He is benign, except sometimes...
when his temper is unshakable.

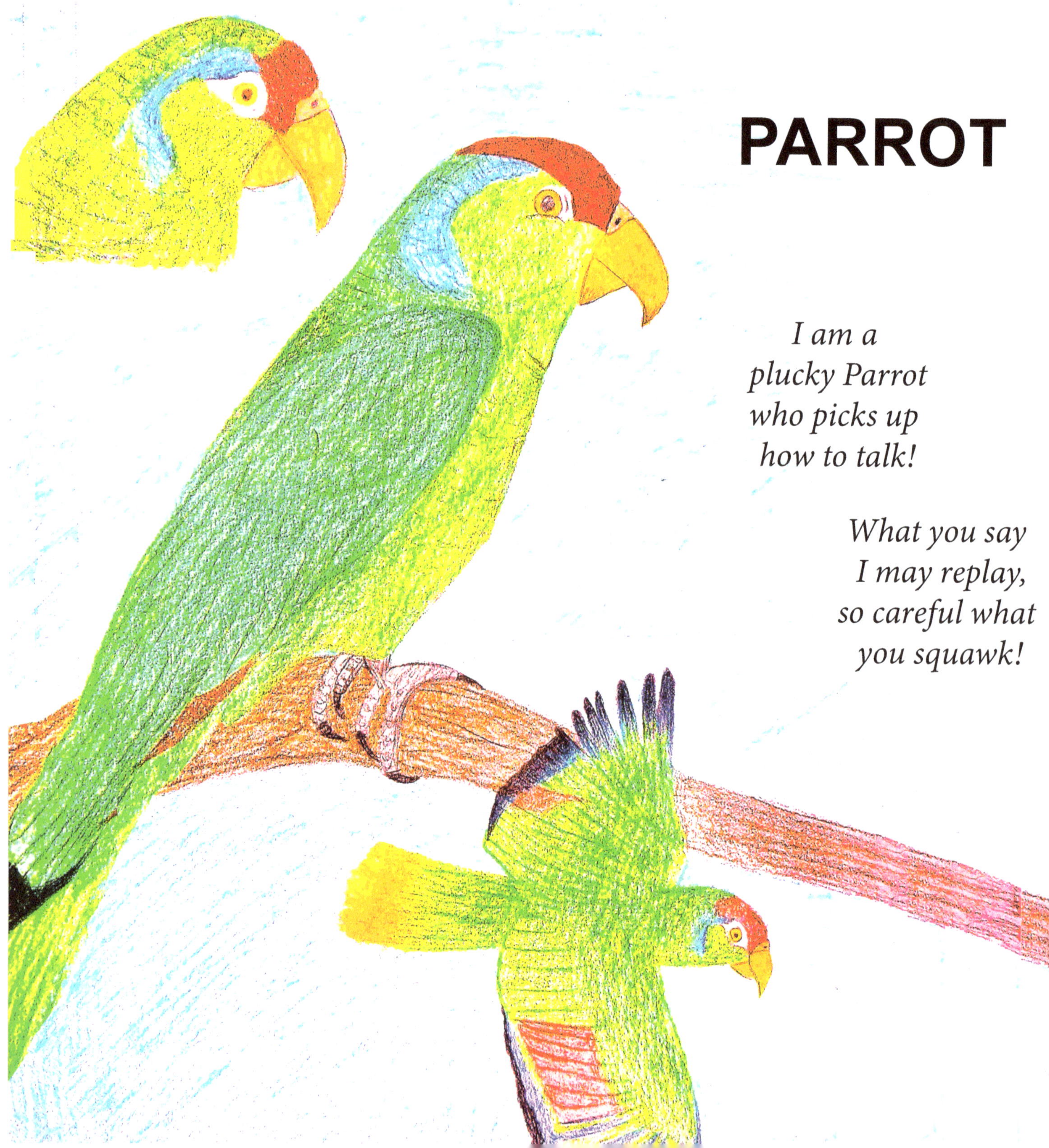

PARROT

I am a
plucky Parrot
who picks up
how to talk!

What you say
I may replay,
so careful what
you squawk!

MAHI
MAHI

I am the Mahi Mahi!
Bull-headed, strong,
and free.
I fight and swim
from what's within -
I'll make you
remember me.

In salty days of December,
in the marsh Carolina brush,
if you slow your boat along the water
and wait there long enough...

You'll find the face of love's first touch,
as it helps make new life breathe!
With great care, moms lift to air
baby Dolphins from the sea!

BOTTLENOSE DOLPHIN

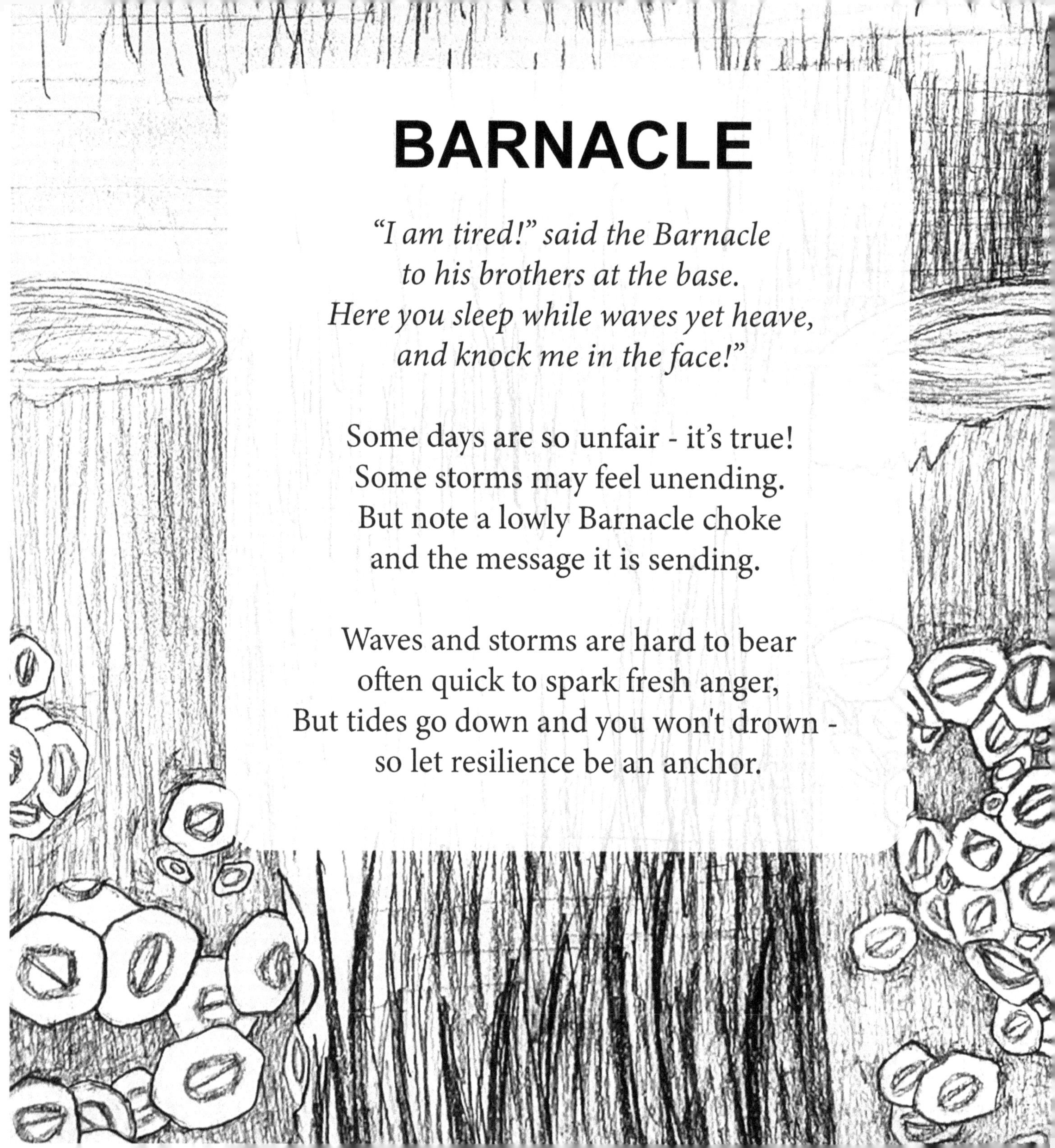

BARNACLE

"I am tired!" said the Barnacle
to his brothers at the base.
Here you sleep while waves yet heave,
and knock me in the face!"

Some days are so unfair - it's true!
Some storms may feel unending.
But note a lowly Barnacle choke
and the message it is sending.

Waves and storms are hard to bear
often quick to spark fresh anger,
But tides go down and you won't drown -
so let resilience be an anchor.

Just like the sweet Black Sea Bass
on coast channels swimming free.
I'll shed all scales dull and pale
to shine bright and bluish-green.

OYSTER

In the age of endless sunsets
when all Oysters had black pearls,
The deep and dark were tasked with balance
throughout this stretch of world.

Should you see a Jimmy Crab
    with legs as blue as ice...
Beware his spiny pincers there -
    you'll find he is not nice!

JIMMY
CRAB

He does not like new visitors,
    he prefers a barren beach...
Don't leave him be and you will see
    the method of his speech!

SPOTTED SEA TROUT

I am a Spotted Sea Trout,
so docile and so sweet!
I swim a lot, have speckled dots
with tasty meat to eat!

In waters fresh I call my home,
for five long years until
I swim upstream to salty seas
to live out my life's fill.

WILD HORSES
When you need
to find the wild
lost deep down
in your soul...
Follow the dawn
down to Corolla
where Wild Horses
are on patrol.

There is a tale of mermaids
now lost to froth and air…
When they used to sun
these sandbars
and wash salt out
from their hair.

Many saw
the mermaids there
and word began to spread…
Fish-like beauties
beyond compare!
Some blue or white or red.

Nature feared
the eyes of men
if more
witnessed the myth...
So she sent a flood
to nip the bud,
and the ocean it did shift!

JINGLE SHELLS

Behold the mermaid's toenails!
Many upon the sand.
A welcome sight to visitors
or natives of this land.

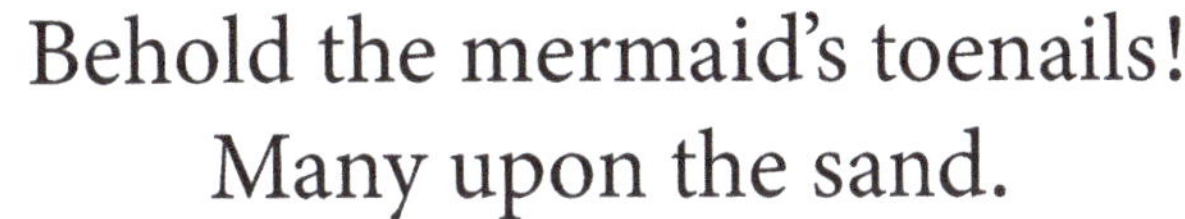

Gaze upon
a Jingle Shell
when your heart is
feeling lost,
to bring back more
along the shore -
of all that time
has cost.

When I need to have a laugh
or remember who I am,
I find the tides or go lakeside
to find my favorite gem.

SWALLOW

When you see her sail the sky,
know she's just begun.
She likes the glide, enjoys the ride -
the Swallow flies for fun.

I feel like the Lavender
Who smells so light and sweet!
Sweet devotion along the ocean
despite the salty sea.

When I need to clear the air
or soothe my inner peace,
I'll call on her, the Lavender,
for anxiety's release.

LAVENDER

I call upon the Angel Oak,
protected and divine!
Hear my heart call out for you
with each word in this rhyme.

I sing this song like whispered wind
to echo in your limbs,
Make me strong,
forgive my wrongs -
by way this passing hymn.

Beneath your shade, I'll find peace,
safe harbor is your gift!
I am renewed in gratitude
because we both exist.

ANGEL OAK

Will you help me, Sea Star,
regrow from what's within?
As we touch, I know this much…
true healing can begin.

STARFISH

When it comes to Lionfish,
look before you trek!
In his spines, a harsh design
that hurt upon misstep.

Also known as a Rockfish,
he blends into the floor.
In warm seas, be careful please!
Should you go explore.

LIONFISH

Come down to the Caribbean
where waters are so warm,
to find a welcome jokester
and ask him to perform...

Tell us a joke, sir Clownfish!
Make known your daily glee!
A proper laugh is all we ask
to leave your anemone.

CLOWNFISH

LINED SEAHORSE

In warm summer shallows,
are two lovers from the sea.
Once they pair in waters there,
neither of them leave.

Should I find
my anchor's match,
I'll call out to ocean's force:
*Bring to me monogamy
akin the
Lined Seahorse!*

There is a sunny flower
    you think is just a weed,
but when it comes to Dandelions
there's much to know indeed.

Used by coastal healers
    for their gifts of medicine;
seeds like stars,
    moon of the marsh,
found where life begins.

DANDELION

BLACK-BACKED
SEAGULL

Have you heard the Black-Backed Gull
calling out above the beach?
He wants your lunch, but know this much...
He's louder with each feast.

There is a friend most holy
that's rare along this sea…
In times when he was gracious,
friendship betrayed him carelessly.

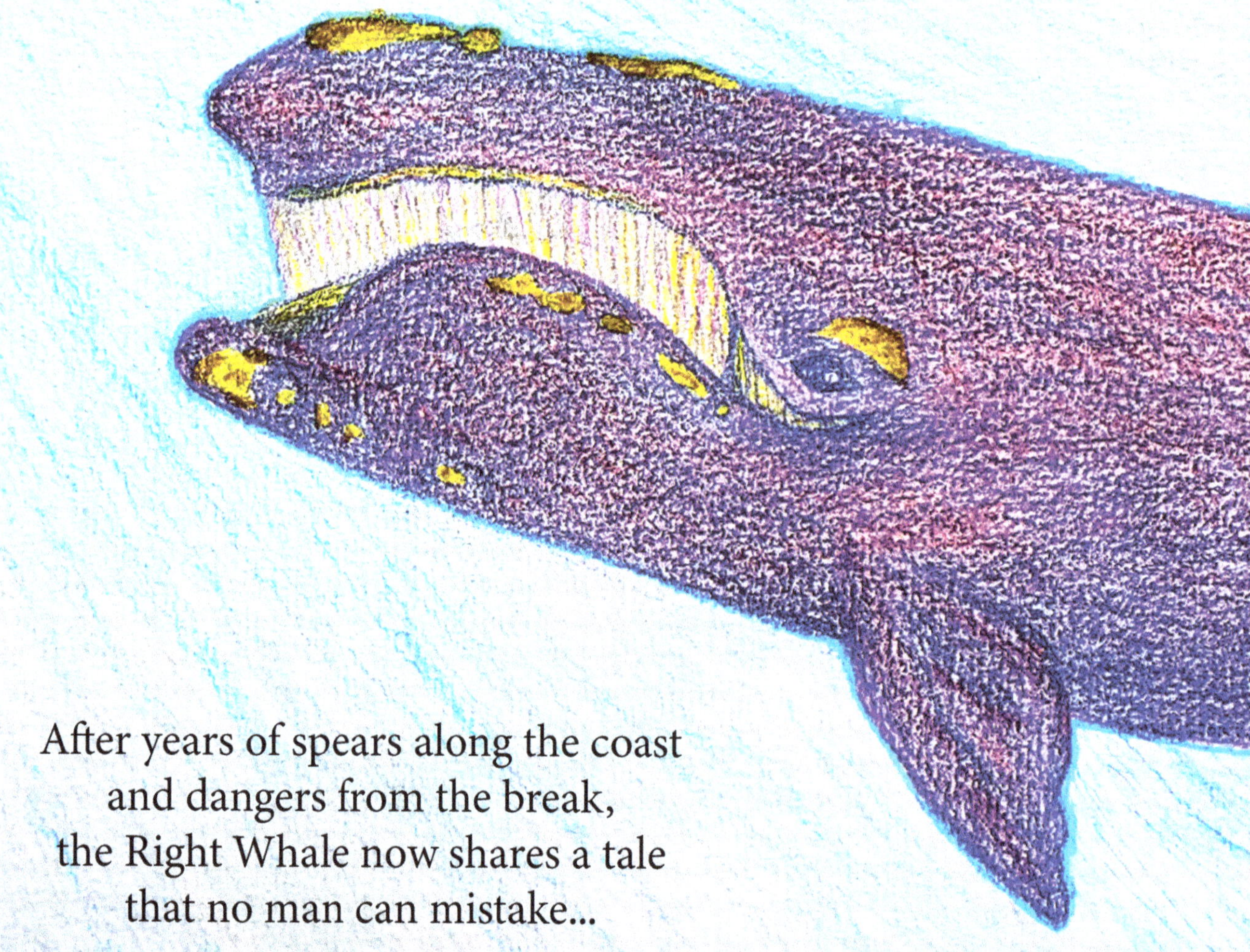

After years of spears along the coast
and dangers from the break,
the Right Whale now shares a tale
that no man can mistake…

My back my bare old battered scars
from the boats and spears above.
My heart may be a broken mess
betrayed by friends or love...

But despite fear, should one appear,
the scars along my hide
show off life's strife, so I invite
a new boat with the next tide.

RIGHT WHALE

Have you seen the sea kelp
that grows in salty seas?
There is a love from those above
that flows below the leaves.

Check out this Otter mother
who floats beneath her pup!
They will hold hands
as love expands,
just like the love in us.

OTTER

Make me like
the Hermit Crab,
in an ever-changing hull!
He can conceive
when best to leave
because it's time to grow.

So if I find another life
big enough to hold my dreams,
I will move on
to a new dawn
because I will believe.

HERMIT
CRAB

RED HAWK

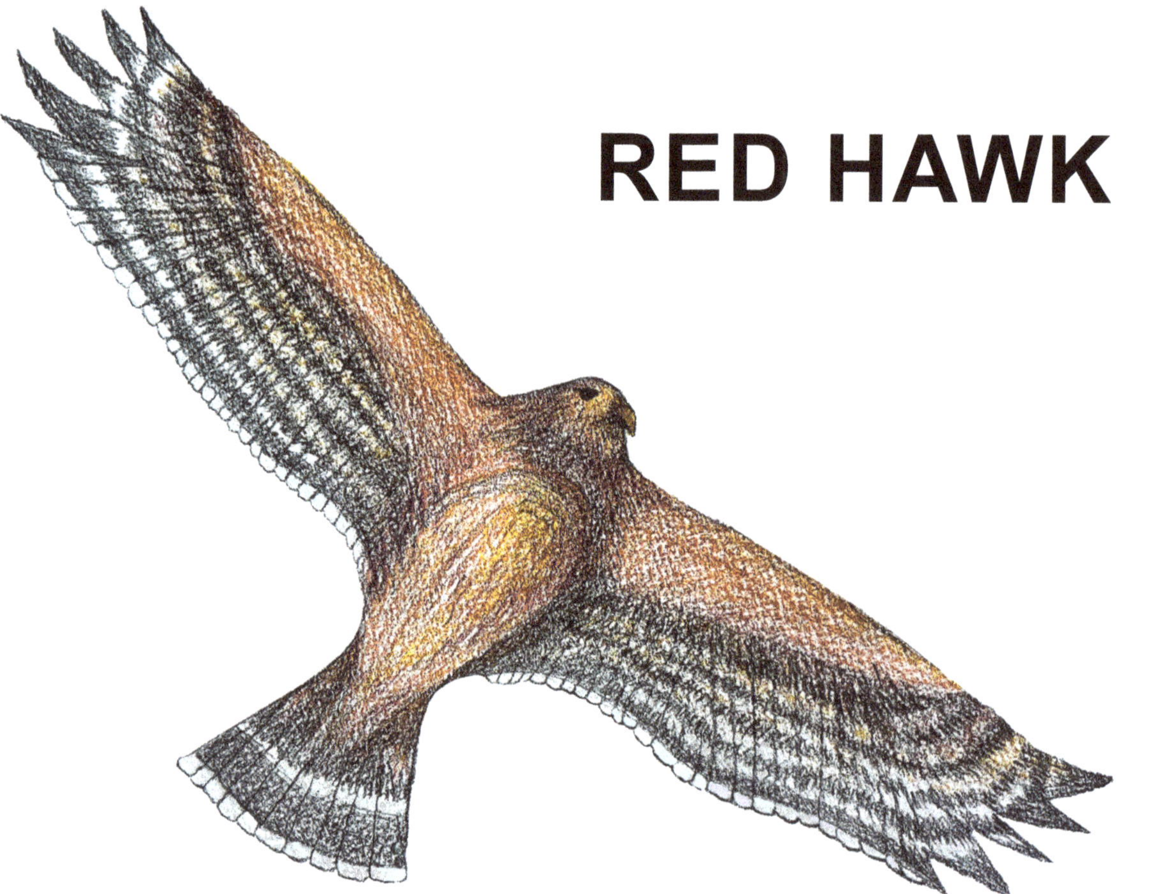

Look above for watchers!
They are known to see...
They keep their eyes on all mankind
and those who breathe beneath.

Among the feathered guardians
that watch us from the sky,
take note the cunning Red Hawk
should she ever catch your eye.

Just like the meek Marsh Rabbit
  who runs before defeat,
I will run fast
    despite sandblasts!
I swear by each heartbeat.

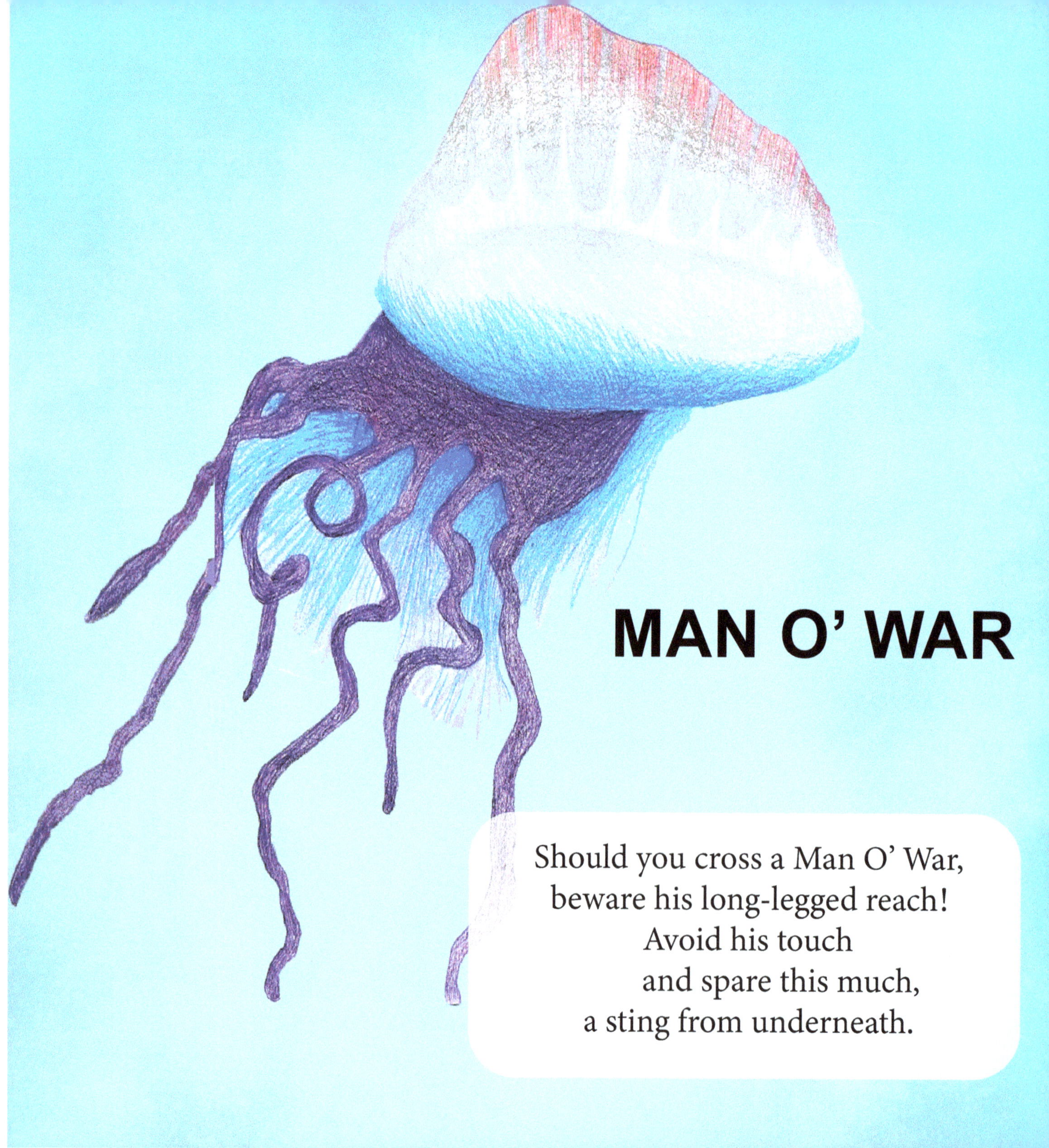

Should you cross a Man O' War,
beware his long-legged reach!
Avoid his touch
and spare this much,
a sting from underneath.

When you want to find new peace
unsure of what's to come...
Look for a sign,
goodness defined
in tides where you belong.

Should you see
an Egret there
above the
morning marsh,
know in your heart,
you can restart
protected by her watch.

EGRET

GREAT WHITE SHARK

Behold a Great White Shark,
who prowls the big, wide blue!
What he wants is sure to haunt
the dreams of me or you.

SAILFISH

I salute to you, O' Sailfish!
Instill in me your speed.
You are the one I need to be,
if I am to succeed.

CAROLINA WREN

I am a Carolina Wren
in the hardy months of winter.
I seem so small and frail to you
like my wings should freeze and splinter.

But each year, I don't fly north
or change how I live or eat…
Perseverance isn't about *what* you are,
It's about *who* you are beneath.

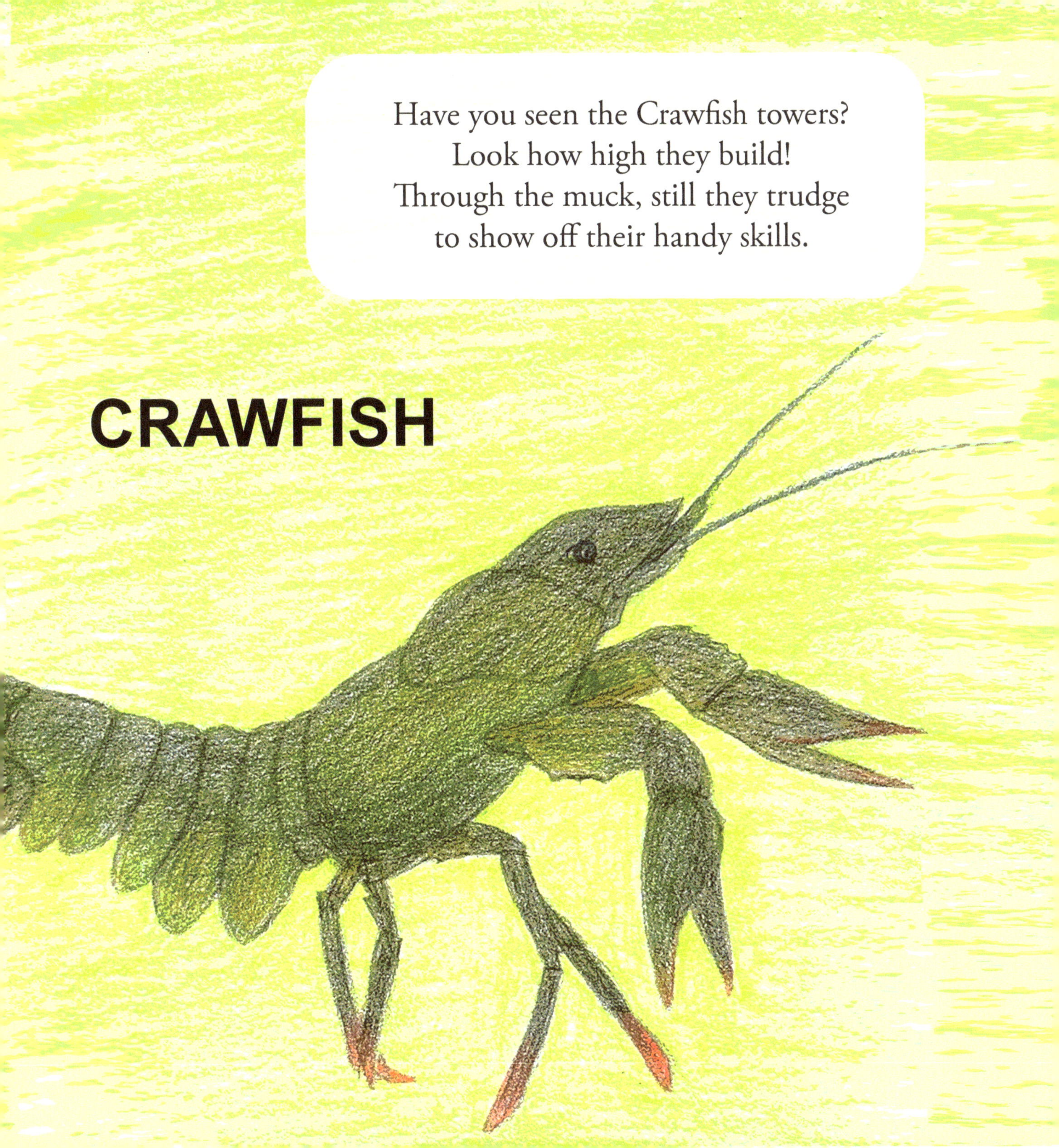

Have you seen the Crawfish towers?
Look how high they build!
Through the muck, still they trudge
to show off their handy skills.

CRAWFISH

DUNEGRASS

I am like the Dunegrass,
that tosses in a storm…
The world may thrash around me,
but beneath is where I'm strong!

Be still the waves inside my head,
let go my rigid spine.
I'll bend beneath
and try to breathe...
I'm flexible by design.

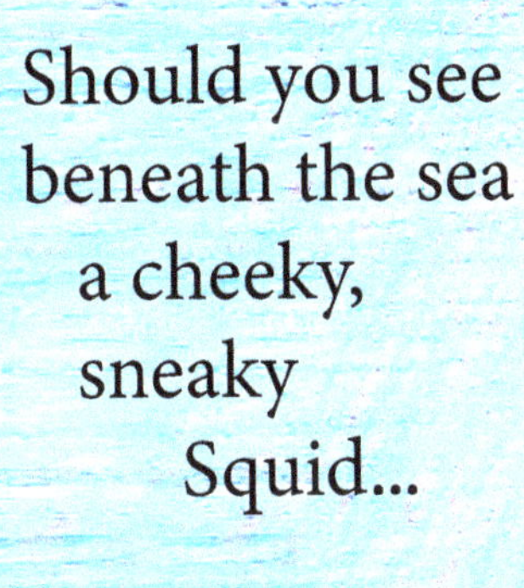

Should you see
beneath the sea
    a cheeky,
    sneaky
        Squid...

You have
her trust
from your
conduct!
Or else
she would
    have hid.

Say hello
but let her go...
the Squid is
very smart!

SQUID

She'll shift
her skin
or hide
from men,
    spray her
        ink, or
        dart.

According to Timucua,
a symbol of new hope...
Known to warn
of impending storms
by being the first to go.

But when those storms
have reached an end,
she'll be the first to fly!
Safe from rain,
post hurricane -
the Ibis is a guid

IBIS

In chilly Arctic waters
lives a happy, snowy friend.
The Beluga Whale is very pale
but her smile never ends.

**BELUGA
WHALE**

Have you seen the Swallowtail
on a Sunday afternoon?
Flower lover like no other,
floating on sand dunes.

SWALLOWTAIL

I am a little Rockhopper
who lives in Arctic seas!
Why not come south
to Cape Horn's mouth
to hop and play with me?
PENGUIN
I can't run fast
or fly away,
but I'm not afraid
of cliffs!
I like to dive
and socialize
on rocks where
Penguins live.

These are soft-shelled Leatherbacks!
with blackened leather legs.
They use the moon in this lagoon
to hatch and lay their eggs.

I'll look for them in summer,
when they've travelled quite a way.
It'll take two years to reappear,
so I'm honored that they came.

LEATHERBACK TURTLE

GREEN FROG

There is a sound deep in the marsh
in summer you may hear...
When the Green Frog croaks, you'll surely know
new eggs will soon appear.

Beware the sneaky Water Snake,
with venom in her mouth!
She can swim and so therein
is dangerous no doubt!

WATER SNAKE

HONEY BEE

When I see the Honey Bee,
I'll know he is a sign.
Like key of C in harmony,
we vibrate by design.

When I hear his beating wings,
my heart beats back its hum!
May I be struck with great new luck
whenever I see one.

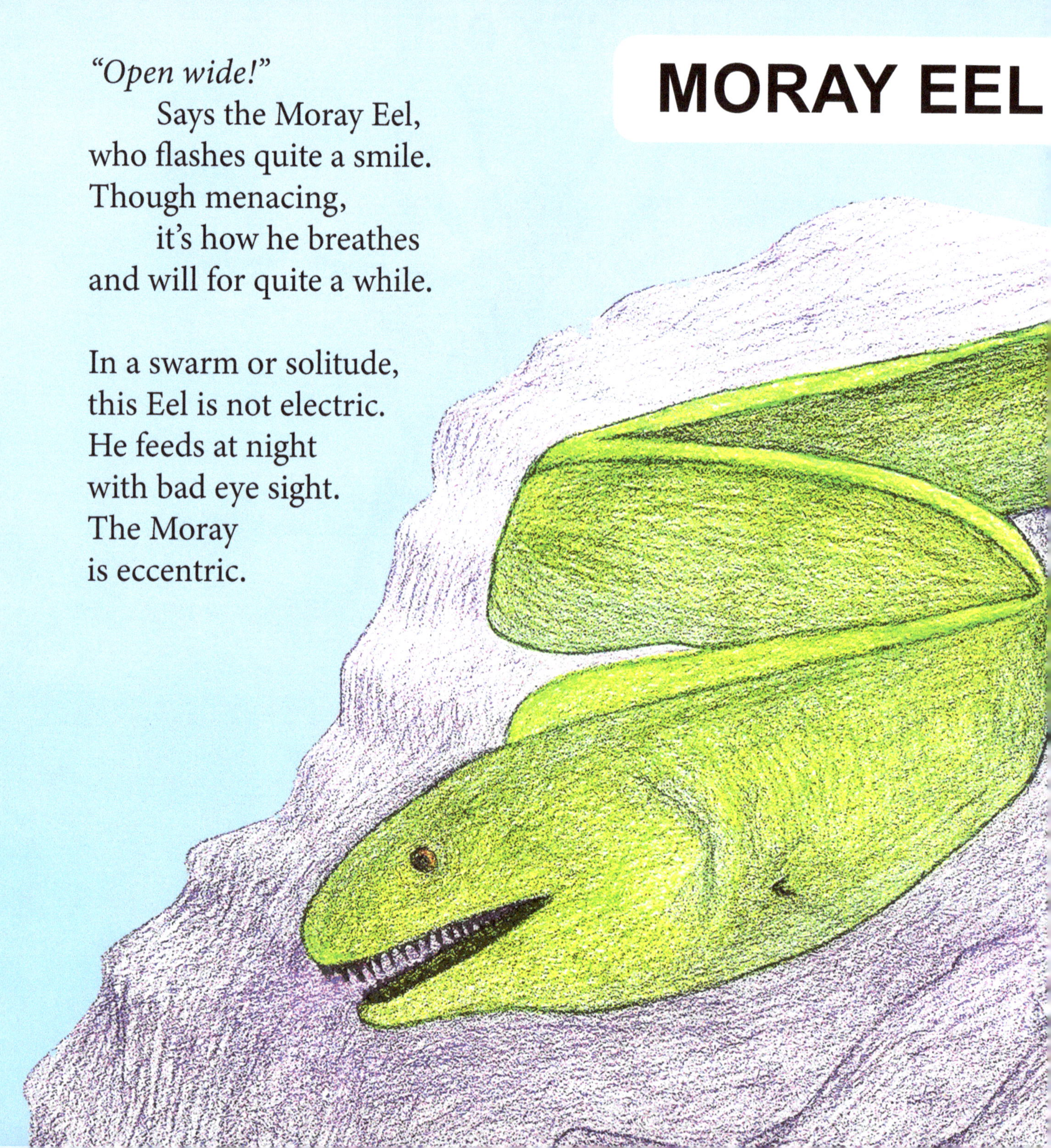

"Open wide!"
  Says the Moray Eel,
who flashes quite a smile.
Though menacing,
  it's how he breathes
and will for quite a while.

In a swarm or solitude,
this Eel is not electric.
He feeds at night
with bad eye sight.
The Moray
is eccentric.

SANDPIPER

Hello, little teeter-peep,
who glides along the sand!
With your long beak
and little squeak,
I am your biggest fan.

I'll do my best to smile back
at your movements ever-hyper…
a small crusader, this little wader!
The plucky, plump Sandpiper.

The Pacific islands harbor treasure
marked by beauty,
        across time
Bright-colored lights,
        the shore's delight -
        these flowers so divine.

Should you want
to find romance,
remember the Hibiscus!

Growing bright and
    then by night
        lost like
        love's
            first kiss.

HIBISCUS

URCHIN

Cast a shadow on an Urchin
and he'll set his spines to fight!
An all-seeing eye of the world around him,
but ever-afraid of night.

I am the elusive Octopus,
      cautious and unarmed.
Survival is my
      spirit guide;
protecting
      me from harm.

When I'm backed
against all odds
I'll manipulate
my hide,

With good cause
and camoflauge
      I'll escape
      again
         this time!

OCTOPUS

STUMPKNOCKER

I channel now the ocean wide,
who speaks to me in sleep!
I know that she wants more from me,
I hear her in the trees.

Make me as the Stumpknocker -
who knows not what he does...
With his eyes, I might surprise.
Not knowing why - because.

There is a burrow guardian
some consider a monstrosity…
As a hunter (not a weaver),
She is nature's curiosity.

WOLF
SPIDER

When you go to Florida,
    find dinosaurs from fiction!
In Belize, they like to tease
    and call them bamboo chickens.

    The Iguana is no enemy
        it prefers to tan or climb.
        They like the sun,
            are quick to run
        and shed their skin sometimes.

IGUANA

Behold the lofty Lichen
who clings to the Oak tree!
Not a vine - an epiphyte.
He grows there graciously.

LICHEN

On branches of the humble Oak
is where he hangs his fate,
And to this day, still lays display
as mark of heaven's gates.

Have you met the Narwhal
who lives where it is cold?
She has a horn like a unicorn
or so the stories go.

SAND DOLLAR

Should you find
a Sand Dollar
left over on the beach,
make sure it's white
or it's still alive!
Remember from this speech.

MOSQUITO

In hot springs or summers,
you'll recognize this pest!
Hard to ignore, along the shore
or wherever it is wet!

Mistaken for the eagle
who lives along the coast,
the Osprey is a native
who soars above
the boats.

To rise just as the Osprey
I must be true and bold!
I let free all I can be.
Let destiny unfold!

OSPREY

Old pirates like to tell a tale
of angels in the deep...
when sailors' graves loomed in the waves
or fate was looking bleak.

Known to travel in great pods -
as they play or swim or jump!
But on bad days, the sailors say,
Striped Dolphins help the lost.

So if you see their dorsal fins,
make sure to act impressed!
Their good heart is due in part
to Isles of the Blessed.

STRIPED DOLPHIN

Make me like the Gray Fox,
with a mind so swift and cunning.
My eyes as fast
    as springtime grass,
words clever and becoming.

GRAY FOX

A cheery coastal neighbor
of the people in the South,
is a friendly springtime visitor
who likes to fly about!

It is the Eastern Bluebird
with feathers so azure!
Aloft in flight, a welcome sight
for all its blue glamour.

EASTERN
BLUEBIRD

NETTLE

Look for weightless
glowing light
beneath
the deep, dark gloom.
With a Nettle's lens,
light may bend
and in life,
your light resume.

On a sunny afternoon
at the edge of shoreline woods,
is an ancient Roman lesson
from the pains of ancient Good.

I am a flowering Dogwood Tree -
disgraced by old defeats!
I'll twist my vines and so in time,
protect my peace beneath.

DOGWOOD
TREE

When I see the Laughing Gulls
high above the marsh,
their familiar call
and southern drawl
make light my
wearied heart.

LAUGHING GULL

They laugh all day
along the shore.
They fly beside
their friends.
I'll laugh along
with my heartsong,
until next summer's end.

Loyal as a Sea Dog
laying in the lonley sun...
When alone, still I know
I will find someone.
I'll dive great depths
to help my friends!
I'll play all day in kind!
Until that day, I'll find a way
to reach them in due time.
SEAL

There is a prize of Aztecs
found along the shore...
a sacred shell,
they used to tell
when the Wind God
was at war.

He took the Conch
into his hands.
The goal to raise alarm...
May all be warned
upon my horn
of all impending harm!

From oceans wide, I call to you -
Please send your humble aid!
Sand to kelp,
I need your help
if I am to be saved.

CONCH

I like to see the Warbler,
who hops along the ground.
He leads the way
and likes to play
wherever he is found!

WARBLER

I like his yellow feathers
or the smile on his face.
When outside, I feel alive!
So I'll hop along in pace.

In fresh and salty waters
waiting just beneath the blue,
is the fairly scary Bull Shark,
who could catch up to you.

BULL SHARK

MAGNOLIA TREE

Did you know the Magnolia Tree
is planted for good luck?
Smelling sweet, she is a treat
that all are sure to love.

SKATE

I look out for the gentle Skate!
She doesn't mind my touch.
Though her skin is slippery,
I know it is quite tough.

Salutations to the Blackfish -
Lord of the ice and sea!
They are quite large and still in charge,
some native men believe.

Often told in legends
for their power and their strength,
echolocate to communicate -
on the Orca's own wavelength.

ORCAS

Vibrate like a Red Drum
and feel his steady beat!
He is renowned all over town
for the sounds that he excretes.

Find him with his reddish scales
or spots along his tail.
Early fall's a free-for-all,
to catch this little male.

RED DRUM

Pleasant as a Whale Shark
with his polka-dotted back!
His perception - electroreception;
in warm waters where he basks.

The biggest fish in the sea
and yet a life benign.
A friend of men and time again
true pleasantness defined.

WHALE SHARK

Find yourself a hollow
where the Catawba
cried out to the dark...
By summer's night,
let free your light
and ignite its
forgotten spark.

FIREFLIES

As you watch the Fireflies glow
flashing on summer skin,
find delight in their twilight
restoring light within.

Hello humble Hummingbird,
who lives along the coast!
You are small and do enthrall
spectators young and old.

My wings are fast,
my diet sweet
I am a happy friend,
Upon my flight,
a joyous sight!
Good fortune is omen.

HUMMINGBIRD

When the White-Tail gather,
it's a sign of certain peace.
It's very rare to see them there
together on the beach.

WHITE-TAIL
DEER

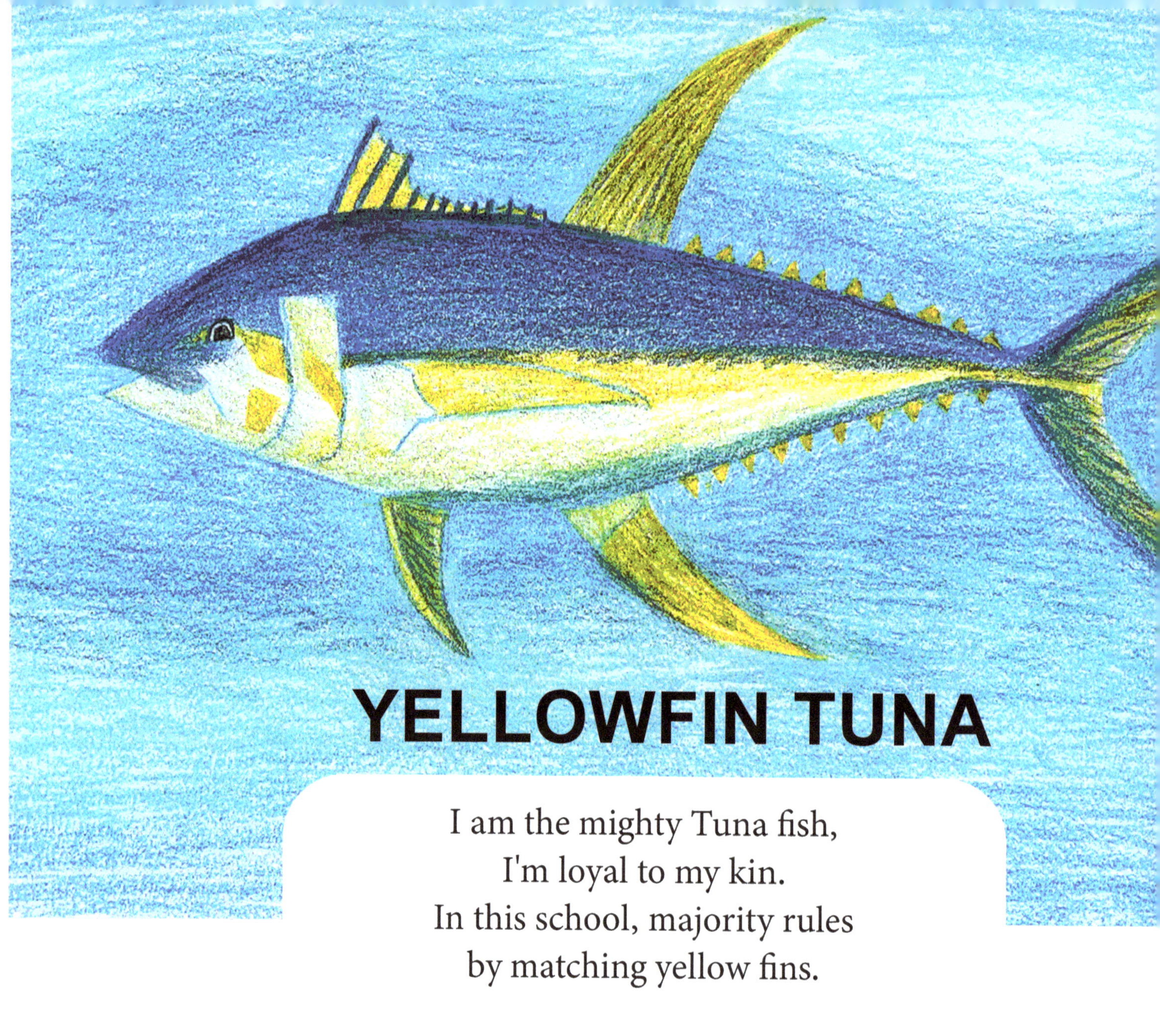

YELLOWFIN TUNA

I am the mighty Tuna fish,
I'm loyal to my kin.
In this school, majority rules
by matching yellow fins.

We swim all day without delay
inside the cold, dark blue!
We have strength to swim great lengths
and some say tasty too!

Beyond our coastal waters
where the oceans open up,
is a trophy prized
by many eyes
with a sword hard
to rebuff.

Make me like the Marlin -
the best at my own skills!
With no contest, I'll be the best.
My dreams I shall fulfill!

LOBSTER

Have you seen
the Lobster
along the
ocean floor?
It is a prize
in many eyes
to spot this
omnivore.

TORTOISE

I am a cheerful Tortoise
who only lives in sand!
I may be slow but still I know
exactly who I am.

With a hard shell and scaly skin
I live for many years.
From creep to clutch - I know this much
my wisdom perseveres.

PELICAN

Along the coast,
    they sail the sky
to spot their next big feast...
But over time,
    Pelicans go blind
for the hunting
    they complete.

Stubborn as a Zebra Shark
who swims against the current.
She hunts at night and has no stripes,
but that is no deterrent.

PUFFERFISH

If you scare a Puffer Fish
he'll inflate like a balloon.
You may not like his pointy spikes
or the look of this odd loon.

WATER LILY

On the surface,
by light they bloom,
fighting all the way
through the dark!
Just like a wily Water Lily…
success is a work of heart.

Beware the tale of U'gal'u
from the ancient Cherokee...
A cautious tale about prevail,
but cost of victory.

There was a tribe
        in the brier patch
plagued by a flying beast.
It picked up children,
        was a villain
        and dined as morning feast.

        Many times the hunters tried,
        to catch the Yellow Jacket!
        But then one day they found a way
        to stop its nasty habit.

                They built a fire out of brush...
                and smoke claimed all within!
                Burning faces to save a race's,
                        but a grave and lasting sin.

As the smoke destroyed
all below -
a new age for us unfurled!
While the last Yellow Jackets
left overhead,
flew away and hid
across the world.
YELLOW JACKET

SALAMANDER

Behold the feeble Fire Lizard
named by the ancient Greeks!
When it gets hot, she runs a lot,
but always comes in peace.

She likes to hide where it is wet;
in marshlands by the sea…
The Salamander is a bystander
so handle carefully.

HORSESHOE CRAB

When the moon
looms overhead
on the coast well after dark,
Look to the sea
to find one of me:
shadow of an armored heart.

I am the hearty Horseshoe Crab
and I prefer to be alone...
except in May or mating day,
I'm safer on my own.

When in need of rescue
but wickedness abounds...
The Maori tell a story
of a time when it was found.

Two brothers torn
by jealousy;
grown up
        beside the sea…
        One benign
        and one unkind
                yet still a family.

With promise
        of a fishing trip
the evil one did lure,
his brother and many others
to a location most obscure.

HUMPBACK WHALE

And there his evil plan took place
as he sunk all their canoes!
Many drowned beneath his bow
forever lost into the blue.

The good brother tread water,
but grew tired beneath the waves.
He cried out to ancient water spirits
and prayed he could be saved.

As his legs began to fail,
a Humpback Whale appeared!
With invitation it did take him
to shore and interfered.

So a message from the *taniwha*,
the humble guardians of earth:
When you need most rescue
pray for magic
in the mirth.

There is a point in every life
when time itself stands still...
You catch your breath, but don't contest
this rare and special thrill.

Should this king loom overhead,
watch where his shadow casts!
From his view, the Eagle too,
can see a higher path.

BALD
EAGLE

QUAHOG

Learn a little lesson
from this creature with assurance:
No matter how the waves may break
the Quahog knows endurance!

Pluck a mollusk from the silt,
and trace along its shell.
Confide in him your every whim
to activate his spell.

DRAGONFLY

When your spirits need a lift
or your heart is feeling stuck,
a Dragonfly could change your ride
as it can bring you luck.

A happy little Walrus
laying on the ice...
He'll stay that way for most the day,
or one-third of his life.

With his large tusks and lots of fat,
he's not afraid of winter.
And in the sun, with his weapons,
he's an impressive swimmer.

I call to me the crestfallen moon,
who cries out to the Atlantic...
free to be anything she wants,
but a hopelessly lost romantic.

To shed old skins and start anew,
I'll endeavor new dedication...
To change my life and reshape my light,
I must channel transformation.

INDEX